Contents

32

46

62

Classic Creations

Lemony Pound Cake

- 1 package (4-serving size) lemon-flavor gelatin
- ¾ cup boiling water
- 1 package **DUNCAN HINES® Moist Deluxe® Classic Yellow Cake Mix**
- 4 eggs
- ¾ cup vegetable oil
- 1 can (6 ounces) frozen lemonade concentrate, thawed
- ½ cup granulated sugar

1. Preheat oven to 350°F. Grease and flour 10-inch tube pan.

2. Dissolve gelatin in water in large mixing bowl; cool. Stir in cake mix, eggs and oil. Beat at medium speed with electric mixer 2 minutes. Spoon into prepared pan. Bake 50 minutes or until toothpick inserted into center comes out clean. Mix lemonade concentrate and sugar in small bowl. Pour over hot cake; cool in pan 1 hour. Remove from pan. Cool completely.

Makes 12 to 16 servings

 Tip *Serve this cake with fresh or thawed frozen strawberries for a special dessert.*

Hummingbird Cake

1 package **DUNCAN HINES®** Moist Deluxe®
  Classic Yellow Cake Mix

1 package (4-serving size) vanilla-flavor
  instant pudding and pie filling mix

½ cup vegetable oil

1 can (8 ounces) crushed pineapple,
  well drained (reserve juice)

Reserved pineapple juice plus
  water to equal 1 cup

4 eggs

1 teaspoon ground cinnamon

½ medium-size ripe banana, cut up

½ cup finely chopped pecans

¼ cup chopped maraschino
  cherries, well drained

Confectioners' sugar

1. Preheat oven to 350°F. Grease and flour 10-inch bundt or tube pan.

2. Combine cake mix, pudding mix, oil, pineapple, 1 cup juice and water mixture, eggs and cinnamon in large bowl. Beat at low speed with electric mixer until moistened. Beat at medium speed 2 minutes. Stir in banana, pecans and cherries. Pour into pan. Bake 50 to 60 minutes or until toothpick inserted into center comes out clean. Cool in pan 25 minutes. Invert onto serving plate. Sprinkle with confectioners' sugar.

Makes 12 to 16 servings

Tip
This cake is also great with Cream Cheese Glaze. For glaze, heat 1 container Duncan Hines® Creamy Home-Style Cream Cheese Frosting in microwave on HIGH (100% power) 30 seconds. Do not overheat. Stir until smooth. Drizzle over cake.

Carrot Layer Cake

Cake

1   package **DUNCAN HINES®** Moist Deluxe®
     Classic Yellow Cake Mix

4   eggs

½   cup vegetable oil

3   cups grated carrots

1   cup finely chopped nuts

2   teaspoons ground cinnamon

Cream Cheese Frosting

1   package (8 ounces) cream cheese, softened

¼   cup (½ stick) butter or margarine, softened

2   teaspoons vanilla extract

4   cups confectioners' sugar

    Whole pecans, for garnish (optional)

1. Preheat oven to 350°F. Grease and flour two 8- or 9-inch round cake pans.

2. For cake, combine cake mix, eggs, oil, carrots, nuts and cinnamon in large bowl. Beat at low speed with electric mixer until moistened. Beat at medium speed 2 minutes. Pour into prepared pans. Bake 35 to 40 minutes or until toothpick inserted into centers comes out clean. Cool.

3. For cream cheese frosting, place cream cheese, butter and vanilla extract into large bowl. Beat at low speed until smooth and creamy. Add confectioners' sugar gradually, beating until smooth. Add more sugar to thicken, or add milk or water to thin frosting, as needed. Fill and frost cooled cake. Garnish with whole pecans, if desired.

Makes 12 to 16 servings

Pineapple Upside-Down Cake

Topping

- ½ cup (1 stick) butter or margarine
- 1 cup firmly packed brown sugar
- 1 can (20 ounces) pineapple slices, well drained
  Maraschino cherries, drained and halved
  Walnut halves

Cake

- 1 package **DUNCAN HINES®** Moist Deluxe® Pineapple Supreme Cake Mix
- 1 package (4-serving size) vanilla-flavor instant pudding and pie filling mix
- 4 eggs
- 1 cup water
- ½ cup oil

1. Preheat oven to 350°F.

2. For topping, melt butter over low heat in 12-inch cast-iron skillet or skillet with ovenproof handle. Remove from heat. Stir in brown sugar. Spread to cover bottom of skillet. Arrange pineapple slices, maraschino cherries and walnut halves in skillet. Set aside.

3. For cake, combine cake mix, pudding mix, eggs, water and oil in large mixing bowl. Beat at medium speed with electric mixer 2 minutes. Pour batter evenly over fruit in skillet. Bake 1 hour or until toothpick inserted into center comes out clean. Invert onto serving plate.

Makes 16 to 20 servings

Tip *This cake can be made in a 13×9×2-inch pan. Bake at 350°F for 45 to 55 minutes or until toothpick inserted into center comes out clean. This cake is also delicious using Duncan Hines® Moist Deluxe® Yellow Cake Mix.*

Strawberry Shortcake

Cake

- **1 package DUNCAN HINES® Moist Deluxe® French Vanilla Cake Mix**
- **3 eggs**
- **1¼ cups water**
- **½ cup (1 stick) butter or margarine, softened**

Filling and Topping

- **2 cups whipping cream, chilled**
- **⅓ cup granulated sugar**
- **½ teaspoon vanilla extract**
- **1 quart fresh strawberries, rinsed, drained and sliced**
- **Mint leaves, for garnish (optional)**

1. Preheat oven to 350°F. Grease two 9-inch round cake pans with butter or margarine. Sprinkle bottoms and sides with granulated sugar.

2. For cake, combine cake mix, eggs, water and butter in large bowl. Beat at low speed with electric mixer until moistened. Beat at medium speed 2 minutes. Pour into prepared pans. Bake 30 to 35 minutes or until toothpick inserted into center comes out clean. Cool in pan 10 minutes. Invert onto cooling rack. Cool completely.

3. For filling and topping, place whipping cream, sugar and vanilla extract in large bowl. Beat at high speed with electric mixer until stiff peaks form. Reserve ⅓ cup for garnish. Place one cake layer on serving plate. Spread with half of remaining whipped cream and half of sliced strawberries. Place second cake layer on top of strawberries. Spread with remaining whipped cream and top with remaining strawberries. Dollop with reserved ⅓ cup whipped cream and garnish with mint leaves, if desired. Refrigerate until ready to serve.

Makes 12 servings

Boston Cream Pie

1 package **DUNCAN HINES® Moist Deluxe® Classic Yellow Cake Mix**

2 containers (3½ ounces each) **ready-to-eat vanilla pudding**

1 container **DUNCAN HINES® Creamy Home-Style Classic Chocolate Frosting**

1. Preheat oven to 350°F. Grease and flour two 8- or 9-inch round cake pans.

2. Prepare, bake and cool cakes following package directions for basic recipe.

3. To assemble, place one cake layer on serving plate. Spread vanilla pudding on top of cake. Top with second cake layer. Remove lid and foil top of frosting container. Heat in microwave oven on HIGH (100% power) 25 to 30 seconds. Stir. (Mixture should be thin.) Spread chocolate glaze over top of second cake layer. Refrigerate until ready to serve.

Tip *For a richer flavor, substitute Duncan Hines® Moist Deluxe® Butter Recipe Golden Cake Mix.*

Makes 12 to 16 servings

Black Forest Torte

> 1 package **DUNCAN HINES® Moist Deluxe®
> Dark Chocolate Fudge Cake Mix**
> 2½ cups whipping cream, chilled
> 2½ tablespoons confectioners' sugar
> 1 can (21 ounces) cherry pie filling

1. Preheat oven to 350°F. Grease and flour two 9-inch round cake pans.

2. Prepare, bake and cool cake following package directions for basic recipe.

3. Beat whipping cream in large bowl until soft peaks form. Add confectioners' sugar gradually. Beat until stiff peaks form.

4. To assemble, place one cake layer on serving plate. Spread two-thirds cherry pie filling on cake to within ½ inch of edge. Spread 1½ cups whipped cream mixture over cherry pie filling. Top with second cake layer. Frost sides and top with remaining whipped cream mixture. Spread remaining cherry pie filling on top to within 1 inch of edge. Refrigerate until ready to serve.

*Makes
12 to 16 servings*

Tip *Chill the cherry pie filling for easy spreading on cake. Also, garnish the cake with grated semisweet chocolate or white chocolate curls, if desired.*

Cindy's Fudgy Brownies

1 package (21 ounces) DUNCAN HINES® Family-Style Chewy Fudge Brownie Mix

1 egg

⅓ cup water

⅓ cup vegetable oil

¾ cup semisweet chocolate chips

½ cup chopped pecans

1. Preheat oven to 350°F. Grease bottom only of 13×9×2-inch pan.

2. Combine brownie mix, egg, water and oil in large bowl. Stir with spoon until well blended, about 50 strokes. Stir in chocolate chips. Spread in prepared pan. Sprinkle with pecans. Bake 25 to 28 minutes or until set. Cool completely. Cut into bars.

Makes 24 brownies

Tip *Overbaking brownies will cause them to become dry. Follow the recommended baking times given in recipes closely.*

Fudge Rum Balls

1	package **DUNCAN HINES® Moist Deluxe® Butter Recipe Fudge Cake Mix**
2	cups sifted confectioners' sugar
1	cup finely chopped pecans or walnuts
¼	cup unsweetened cocoa powder
1	tablespoon rum extract
	Pecans or walnuts, finely chopped

1. Preheat oven to 375°F. Grease and flour 13×9×2-inch pan.

2. Prepare, bake and cool cake following package directions for basic recipe.

3. Crumble cake into large bowl. Stir with fork until crumbs are fine and uniform in size. Add confectioners' sugar, 1 cup nuts, cocoa and rum extract. Stir until well blended.

4. Shape heaping tablespoonfuls of mixture into balls. Garnish by rolling balls in finely chopped nuts. Press firmly to adhere nuts.

Makes 6 dozen rum balls

Tip *You can substitute rum for the rum extract.*

Lemon Bars

1 package **DUNCAN HINES®** Moist Deluxe® Lemon Supreme Cake Mix

3 eggs, divided

⅓ cup butter-flavor shortening

½ cup granulated sugar

¼ cup lemon juice

2 teaspoons grated lemon peel

½ teaspoon baking powder

¼ teaspoon salt

Confectioners' sugar

1. Preheat oven to 350°F.

2. Combine cake mix, 1 egg and shortening in large mixing bowl. Beat at low speed with electric mixer until crumbs form. Reserve 1 cup. Pat remaining mixture lightly into ungreased 13×9×2-inch pan. Bake 15 minutes or until lightly browned.

3. Combine remaining 2 eggs, granulated sugar, lemon juice, lemon peel, baking powder and salt in medium mixing bowl. Beat at medium speed with electric mixer until light and foamy. Pour over hot crust. Sprinkle with reserved crumb mixture.

4. Bake 15 minutes longer or until lightly browned. Sprinkle with confectioners' sugar. Cool in pan. Cut into bars.

Makes 30 to 32 bars

 Tip *These bars are also delicious using Duncan Hines® Moist Deluxe® Classic Yellow Cake Mix.*

Holiday Fruit Cake

1	pound diced candied mixed fruits
8	ounces candied cherries, cut into halves
4	ounces candied pineapple, chopped
1½	cups chopped nuts
1	cup raisins
½	cup all-purpose flour
1	package **DUNCAN HINES**® Moist Deluxe® Spice Cake Mix
1	package (4-serving size) vanilla-flavor instant pudding and pie filling mix
3	eggs
½	cup vegetable oil
¼	cup water
	Light corn syrup, heated, for garnish

1. Preheat oven to 300°F. Grease 10-inch tube pan. Line bottom with aluminum foil.

2. Reserve ¼ cup assorted candied fruits and nuts for garnish, if desired. Combine remaining candied fruits, nuts and raisins in large bowl. Toss with flour until evenly coated; set aside.

3. Combine cake mix, pudding mix, eggs, oil and water in large mixing bowl. Beat at medium speed with electric mixer 3 minutes (batter will be very stiff). Stir in candied fruit mixture. Spread in prepared pan. Bake 2 hours or until toothpick inserted into center comes out clean. Cool completely in pan. Invert onto serving plate. Peel off foil.

4. Brush cake with hot corn syrup and decorate with reserved candied fruit pieces and nuts, if desired. To store, wrap in aluminum foil or plastic wrap, or place in airtight container.

Makes 20 to 24 servings

Luscious Layer Cakes

Mocha Fudge Cake

- **1** package **DUNCAN HINES® Moist Deluxe®** **Butter Recipe Fudge Cake Mix**
- **1** tablespoon instant coffee granules
- **1** teaspoon warm water
- **1** cup hot fudge ice cream topping
- **4** cups frozen nondairy whipped topping, thawed, divided

1. Preheat oven to 375°F. Grease and flour two 9-inch round cake pans.

2. Prepare, bake and cool cake following package directions for basic recipe.

3. Combine coffee and water in medium bowl. Stir until coffee crystals are dissolved. Add hot fudge topping and mix well. Fold 2 cups whipped topping into fudge topping mixture. Refrigerate 30 minutes.

4. To assemble, place one cake layer on serving plate. Spread with 1 cup filling. Top with second cake layer. Add remaining 2 cups whipped topping to remaining filling. Frost top and sides of cake with topping mixture.

Makes 12 to 16 servings

Apricot Cream Cake

Cake

- 1   package **DUNCAN HINES®** Moist Deluxe® Classic Yellow Cake Mix
- 1   jar (18 ounces) apricot preserves, divided

Frosting

- 1   package (4-serving size) vanilla-flavor instant pudding and pie filling mix
- ¾   cup milk
- 1½ cups whipping cream, chilled
- ¼   cup toasted flaked coconut, for garnish

  Apricot halves and mint leaves, for garnish (optional)

1. Preheat oven to 350°F. Grease and flour two 9-inch round cake pans.

2. Prepare, bake and cool cake following package directions for basic recipe.

3. To assemble, split each cake layer in half horizontally. Reserve 1 tablespoon preserves. Place one split cake layer on serving plate. Spread one-third remaining preserves on top. Repeat with remaining layers and preserves, leaving top plain.

4. For frosting, prepare pudding mix as directed on package, using ¾ cup milk. Beat whipping cream until stiff in large bowl. Fold whipped cream into pudding. Spread on sides and top of cake. Garnish with coconut, apricot halves and mint leaves. Warm reserved 1 tablespoon preserves to glaze apricot halves. Refrigerate until ready to serve.

Makes 12 to 16 servings

Tip   *You can substitute 3 cups thawed frozen nondairy whipped topping for the whipping cream.*

Chocolate Royale

Cake

1 package **DUNCAN HINES® Moist Deluxe® Devil's Food Cake Mix**

Frosting

1 package (3 ounces) cream cheese, softened
½ cup confectioners' sugar
1 teaspoon vanilla extract
1 cup whipping cream, whipped
2 large bananas, peeled and sliced
Lemon juice
Chocolate sprinkles

1. Preheat oven to 350°F. Grease and flour two 8-inch round cake pans.

2. Prepare, bake and cool cake following package directions for basic recipe.

3. For frosting, combine cream cheese, confectioners' sugar and vanilla extract in small bowl. Beat at low speed with electric mixer until blended. Fold whipped cream into cheese mixture.

4. To assemble, place one cake layer on serving plate. Spread with thin layer of frosting. Reserve 12 banana slices for garnish; dip in lemon juice. Cover frosting with remaining banana slices. Spread another thin layer of frosting over bananas. Place second cake layer on top. Frost sides and top of cake with remaining frosting. Blot reserved banana slices dry on paper towel. Roll banana slices in chocolate sprinkles. Garnish top of cake with banana slices. Refrigerate until ready to serve.

Makes 12 to 16 servings

Strawberry Vanilla Cake

 1 package **DUNCAN HINES® Moist Deluxe® French Vanilla Cake Mix**

 1 container **DUNCAN HINES® Creamy Home-Style Classic Vanilla Frosting, divided**

 ⅓ **cup seedless strawberry jam**

 Fresh strawberries, for garnish (optional)

1. Preheat oven to 350°F. Grease and flour two 8- or 9-inch round cake pans.

2. Prepare, bake and cool cake following package directions for basic recipe.

3. To assemble, place one cake layer on serving plate. Place ¼ cup frosting in small resealable plastic food storage bag. Cut off one corner. Pipe bead of frosting on top of layer around outer edge. Fill remaining area with strawberry jam. Top with second cake layer. Spread remaining frosting on sides and top of cake. Decorate with fresh strawberries, if desired.

Makes 12 to 16 servings

Tip *You can substitute Duncan Hines® French Vanilla or Cream Cheese Frosting, if desired.*

Refreshing Lemon Cake

1 package **DUNCAN HINES®** Moist Deluxe®
   Butter Recipe Golden Cake Mix

1 container **DUNCAN HINES®** Creamy
   Home-Style Cream Cheese Frosting

¾ cup purchased lemon curd

**Lemon drop candies, crushed,
   for garnish (optional)**

1. Preheat oven to 375°F. Grease and flour two 8- or 9-inch round cake pans.

2. Prepare, bake and cool cake following package directions for basic recipe.

3. To assemble, place one cake layer on serving plate. Place ¼ cup frosting in small resealable plastic food storage bag. Cut off one corner. Pipe a bead of frosting on top of layer around outer edge. Fill remaining area with lemon curd. Top with second cake layer. Spread remaining frosting on sides and top of cake. Garnish top of cake with crushed lemon candies, if desired.

Makes 12 to 16 servings

Tip *You can substitute Duncan Hines® Buttercream or Classic Vanilla Frosting, if desired.*

Chocolate Dream Torte

1 package **DUNCAN HINES® Moist Deluxe® Dark Chocolate Fudge Cake Mix**

1 package (6 ounces) **semisweet chocolate chips, melted**

1 container (8 ounces) **frozen nondairy whipped topping, thawed**

1 container **DUNCAN HINES® Creamy Home-Style Milk Chocolate Frosting**

3 tablespoons **finely chopped dry-roasted pistachios**

1. Preheat oven to 350°F. Grease and flour two 9-inch round cake pans.

2. Prepare, bake and cool cake following package directions for basic recipe.

3. For chocolate hearts garnish, spread melted chocolate to 1/8-inch thickness on waxed-paper-lined baking sheet. Cut shapes with heart cookie cutter when chocolate begins to set. Refrigerate until firm. Push out heart shapes. Set aside.

4. To assemble, split each cake layer in half horizontally. Place one split cake layer on serving plate. Spread one-third of whipped topping on top. Repeat with remaining layers and whipped topping, leaving top plain. Frost sides and top with frosting. Sprinkle pistachios on top. Position chocolate hearts by pushing points down into cake. Refrigerate until ready to serve.

Makes 12 to 16 servings

Chocolate Strawberry Dream Torte

Omit semisweet chocolate chips and chopped pistachios. Proceed as directed through step 2. Fold 1 1/2 cups chopped fresh strawberries into whipped topping in large bowl. Assemble as directed, filling torte with strawberry mixture. Frost with milk chocolate frosting, and garnish cake with strawberry fans and mint leaves, if desired.

Banana Fudge Layer Cake

1 package **DUNCAN HINES®** Moist Deluxe® Classic Yellow Cake Mix

1⅓ cups water

3 eggs

⅓ cup vegetable oil

1 cup mashed ripe bananas (about 3 medium)

1 container **DUNCAN HINES®** Creamy Home-Style Classic Chocolate Frosting

1. Preheat oven to 350°F. Grease and flour two 9-inch round cake pans.

2. Combine cake mix, water, eggs and oil in large bowl. Beat at low speed with electric mixer until moistened. Beat at medium speed 2 minutes. Stir in bananas. Pour into prepared pans. Bake 28 to 31 minutes or until toothpick inserted into center comes out clean. Cool in pans 15 minutes. Remove from pans; cool completely.

3. Fill and frost cake with frosting. Garnish as desired.

Makes 12 to 16 servings

Tip *For a richer flavor, substitute Duncan Hines® Moist Deluxe® Butter Recipe Golden Cake Mix.*

Easy Cream Cake

- 1 package **DUNCAN HINES®** Moist Deluxe® Classic White Cake Mix
- 3 egg whites
- 1⅓ cups half-and-half
- 2 tablespoons vegetable oil
- 1 cup flaked coconut, finely chopped
- ½ cup finely chopped pecans
- 2 containers **DUNCAN HINES®** Creamy Home-Style Cream Cheese Frosting

1. Preheat oven to 350°F. Grease and flour three 8-inch round cake pans.

2. Combine cake mix, egg whites, half-and-half, oil, coconut and pecans in large bowl. Beat at low speed with electric mixer until moistened. Beat at medium speed 2 minutes. Pour into prepared pans. Bake 22 to 25 minutes or until toothpick inserted into center comes out clean. Cool, following package directions.

3. To assemble, place one cake layer on serving plate. Spread with ¾ cup frosting. Place second cake layer on top. Spread with ¾ cup frosting. Top with third layer. Spread ¾ cup frosting on top only. Garnish as desired.

Makes 12 to 16 servings

Tip *Spread leftover frosting between two graham crackers for an easy snack.*

Autumn Gold Pumpkin Cake

1 package **DUNCAN HINES® Moist Deluxe® Butter Recipe Golden Cake Mix**

3 eggs

1 cup water

1 cup solid-pack pumpkin

1 ½ teaspoons ground cinnamon, divided

¼ teaspoon ground ginger

¼ teaspoon ground nutmeg

1 cup chopped walnuts

1 container **DUNCAN HINES® Creamy Home-Style Classic Vanilla Frosting**

¼ cup coarsely chopped walnuts, for garnish

1. Preheat oven to 375°F. Grease and flour two 8-inch round cake pans.

2. Combine cake mix, eggs, water, pumpkin, 1 teaspoon cinnamon, ginger and nutmeg in large mixing bowl. Beat at medium speed with electric mixer 4 minutes. Stir in 1 cup walnuts. Pour into prepared pans. Bake 30 to 35 minutes or until toothpick inserted into center comes out clean. Cool in pans 15 minutes. Remove from pans. Cool.

3. Combine frosting and remaining ½ teaspoon cinnamon. Stir until blended. Fill and frost cake. Garnish with ¼ cup walnuts.

Makes 12 to 16 servings

Chocolate Cherry Torte

1 package DUNCAN HINES® Moist Deluxe® Devil's Food Cake Mix

1 can (21 ounces) cherry pie filling

¼ teaspoon almond extract

1 container (8 ounces) frozen nondairy whipped topping, thawed

¼ cup toasted sliced almonds, for garnish (optional)

1. Preheat oven to 350°F. Grease and flour two 9-inch round cake pans.

2. Prepare, bake and cool cake following package directions for basic recipe.

3. Combine cherry pie filling and almond extract in small bowl. Stir until blended.

4. To assemble, place one cake layer on serving plate. Spread with 1 cup whipped topping, then half of cherry pie filling mixture. Top with second cake layer. Spread remaining pie filling to within 1½ inches of cake edge. Decorate cake edge with remaining whipped topping. Garnish with sliced almonds, if desired.

Makes 12 to 16 servings

Tip *To toast almonds, spread in a single layer on baking sheet. Bake at 325°F for 4 to 6 minutes or until fragrant and golden.*

Easy Snack Cakes

Double Fudge Marble Cake

- 1 package **DUNCAN HINES®** Moist Deluxe® Fudge Marble Cake Mix
- 1 container **DUNCAN HINES®** Creamy Home-Style Milk Chocolate Frosting
- ¼ cup hot fudge topping

1. Preheat oven to 350°F. Grease and flour 13×9×2-inch pan.

2. Prepare, bake and cool cake following package directions for basic recipe.

3. Frost top of cooled cake. Place hot fudge topping in small microwave-safe bowl. Microwave on HIGH (100% power) 30 seconds or until thin. Drop hot fudge by spoonfuls on top of cake in 18 places. Pull tip of knife once through each hot fudge dollop to form heart shapes.

Makes 12 to 16 servings

Tip *Hot fudge topping may also be marbled into frosting by using flat blade of knife to swirl slightly.*

Pumpkin Streusel Cake

Streusel

- 1 cup packed brown sugar
- 2 teaspoons ground cinnamon
- ⅓ cup butter or margarine, softened
- 1 cup chopped nuts

Cake

- 1 package **DUNCAN HINES®** Moist Deluxe® Classic Yellow Cake Mix
- 1 can (16 ounces) solid-pack pumpkin
- 3 eggs
- ¼ cup (½ stick) butter or margarine, softened

1. Preheat oven to 350°F.

2. For streusel, combine brown sugar and cinnamon in small bowl. Cut in ⅓ cup butter with pastry blender or 2 knives. Stir in nuts; set aside.

3. For cake, combine cake mix, pumpkin, eggs and ¼ cup butter in large mixing bowl. Beat at medium speed with electric mixer 2 minutes. Spread half of batter into ungreased 13×9×2-inch pan. Sprinkle half of streusel over batter. Spread remaining batter over streusel. Top with remaining streusel. Bake 40 to 45 minutes or until toothpick inserted into center comes out clean.

Makes 12 to 16 servings

Tip *Serve warm as a coffeecake, or cool to serve as a dessert topped with whipped topping.*

Kids' Confetti Cake

Cake

- 1 package **DUNCAN HINES®** Moist Deluxe® Classic Yellow Cake Mix
- 1 package (4-serving size) vanilla-flavor instant pudding and pie filling mix
- 4 eggs
- 1 cup water
- ½ cup vegetable oil
- 1 cup mini semisweet chocolate chips

Topping

- 1 cup colored miniature marshmallows
- ⅔ cup **DUNCAN HINES®** Creamy Home-Style Classic Chocolate Frosting
- 2 tablespoons mini semisweet chocolate chips

1. Preheat oven to 350°F. Grease and flour 13×9×2-inch pan.

2. For cake, combine cake mix, pudding mix, eggs, water and oil in large bowl. Beat at medium speed with electric mixer 2 minutes. Stir in 1 cup chocolate chips. Pour into prepared pan. Bake 40 to 45 minutes or until toothpick inserted into center comes out clean.

3. For topping, immediately arrange marshmallows evenly over hot cake. Place frosting in microwave-safe bowl. Microwave on HIGH (100% power) 25 to 30 seconds. Stir until smooth. Drizzle evenly over marshmallows and cake. Sprinkle with 2 tablespoons chocolate chips. Cool completely.

Makes 12 to 16 servings

Fudge Cake with Melba Topping

Cake

- 1 package **DUNCAN HINES®** Moist Deluxe® Dark Chocolate Fudge Cake Mix
- **Egg substitute product equal to 3 eggs**
- 1¼ cups water
- ½ cup vegetable oil

Melba Topping

- 1 package (12 ounces) frozen dry-pack raspberries, thawed, drained and juice reserved
- ½ cup granulated sugar
- 2 teaspoons cornstarch
- ½ teaspoon grated lemon peel
- 1 can (29 ounces) sliced peaches in light syrup, drained

1. Preheat oven to 350°F. Grease and flour 13×9×2-inch pan.

2. For cake, combine cake mix, egg substitute, water and oil in large bowl. Beat at medium speed with electric mixer 2 minutes. Pour into prepared pan. Bake 35 to 40 minutes or until toothpick inserted into center comes out clean. Cool completely.

3. For topping, combine reserved raspberry juice, sugar, cornstarch and lemon peel in medium saucepan. Bring to a boil. Reduce heat and cook until thickened, stirring constantly. Stir in raspberries. Cool.

4. Cut cake into serving squares. Place several peach slices on top of cake square. Spoon raspberry sauce over peaches and cake. Serve immediately.

Makes 20 servings

Tip *To separate juice from raspberries in one step, allow berries to thaw at room temperature in a strainer placed over a bowl.*

Orange Soak Cake

Cake

> 1 package **DUNCAN HINES®** Moist Deluxe® Orange Supreme Cake Mix

Glaze

> 2 cups confectioners' sugar
>
> ⅓ cup orange juice
>
> 2 tablespoons butter or margarine, melted
>
> 1 tablespoon water

1. Preheat oven to 350°F. Grease and flour 13×9×2-inch pan.

2. For cake, prepare and bake following package directions for basic recipe. Poke holes in top of warm cake with tines of fork or toothpick.

3. For glaze, combine confectioners' sugar, orange juice, melted butter and water in medium bowl. Pour slowly over top of cake, allowing glaze to soak into warm cake. Cool completely.

Makes 12 to 16 servings

 Tip   *For smooth, lump-free pouring, sift confectioners' sugar before preparing glaze.*

Double Chocolate Snack Cake

> 1 package **DUNCAN HINES®** Moist Deluxe®
> Devil's Food Cake Mix
>
> 1 cup white chocolate chips, divided
>
> ½ cup semisweet chocolate chips

1. Preheat oven to 350°F. Grease and flour 13×9×2-inch pan.

2. Prepare cake mix following package directions. Stir in ½ cup white chocolate chips and semisweet chocolate chips. Pour into prepared pan. Bake 35 to 40 minutes or until toothpick inserted into center comes out clean. Remove from oven; sprinkle top with remaining ½ cup white chocolate chips. Serve warm or cool completely in pan.

Makes 12 to 16 servings

Tip
For a special dessert, serve cake warm with a scoop of vanilla ice cream or whipped cream garnished with chocolate chips.

Dump Cake

1 can (20 ounces) crushed pineapple with juice,
    undrained
1 can (21 ounces) cherry pie filling
1 package **DUNCAN HINES®** Moist Deluxe®
    Classic Yellow Cake Mix
1 cup chopped pecans or walnuts
½ cup (1 stick) butter or margarine, cut into
    thin slices

1. Preheat oven to 350°F. Grease 13×9×2-inch pan.

2. Dump pineapple with juice into prepared pan. Spread evenly.
Dump in pie filling. Spread evenly. Sprinkle cake mix evenly over
cherry layer. Sprinkle pecans over cake mix. Dot with butter.
Bake 50 minutes or until top is lightly browned. Serve warm or
at room temperature.

Makes 12 to 16 servings

Tip
*You can substitute Duncan
Hines® Moist Deluxe®
Pineapple Supreme Cake Mix.*

Upside-Down German Chocolate Cake

  1½ **cups flaked coconut**

  1½ **cups chopped pecans**

  1 **package DUNCAN HINES® Moist Deluxe® German Chocolate Cake Mix or Classic Chocolate Cake Mix**

  1 **package (8 ounces) cream cheese, softened**

  ½ **cup (1 stick) butter or margarine, melted**

  1 **pound (3½ to 4 cups) confectioners' sugar**

1. Preheat oven to 350°F. Grease and flour 13×9×2-inch pan.

2. Spread coconut evenly on bottom of prepared pan. Sprinkle with pecans. Prepare cake mix following package directions for basic recipe. Pour over coconut and pecans. Combine cream cheese and melted butter in medium mixing bowl. Beat at low speed with electric mixer until creamy. Add confectioners' sugar; beat until blended and smooth. Drop by spoonfuls evenly over cake batter. Bake 45 to 50 minutes or until toothpick inserted halfway to bottom of cake comes out clean. Cool completely in pan. To serve, cut into individual pieces; turn upside down onto plate.

Makes 12 to 16 servings

Tip *This cake can be served warm, if desired. Also, store leftover coconut in the refrigerator and use within four weeks.*

Cupcake Treats

Rocky Road Cupcakes

- 1 package **DUNCAN HINES®** Moist Deluxe® Devil's Food Cake Mix
- 1 container **DUNCAN HINES®** Creamy Home-Style Classic Vanilla Frosting
- ½ cup creamy peanut butter
- ⅓ cup semisweet chocolate chips
- ⅓ cup salted cocktail peanuts

1. Preheat oven to 350°F. Place paper liners into 24 standard (2½-inch) muffin cups.

2. Prepare, bake and cool cupcakes following package directions.

3. Combine frosting and peanut butter in medium bowl. Frost cupcakes. Sprinkle with chocolate chips and peanuts.

Makes 24 cupcakes

Quick Rocky Road Cake

Grease and flour 13×9×2-inch pan. Prepare, bake and cool cake following package directions for basic recipe. Frost top of cake and garnish as directed above.

Coconut Cupcakes

1   package **DUNCAN HINES®** Moist Deluxe®
       Butter Recipe Golden Cake Mix

3   **eggs**

1   **cup (8 ounces) dairy sour cream**

⅔   **cup cream of coconut**

¼   **cup (½ stick) butter or margarine, softened**

2   **containers (16 ounces each) DUNCAN
       HINES® Creamy Home-Style Coconut
       Supreme Frosting**

Toasted coconut, for garnish (optional)

1. Preheat oven to 375°F. Place paper liners into 36 standard (2½-inch) muffin cups.

2. Combine cake mix, eggs, sour cream, cream of coconut and butter in large bowl. Beat at low speed with electric mixer until blended. Beat at medium speed 4 minutes. Fill paper liners half full. Bake 17 to 19 minutes or until toothpick inserted into centers comes out clean. Cool in pans 5 minutes. Transfer to cooling racks to cool completely. Frost cupcakes. Garnish with toasted coconut.

Makes 36 cupcakes

Tip
To toast coconut, spread evenly on baking sheet. Bake at 350°F for 3 minutes. Stir and bake 1 to 2 minutes longer or until golden brown.

Fudge 'n' Banana Cupcakes

> 1　package **DUNCAN HINES® Moist Deluxe®**
> **Devil's Food Cake Mix**
>
> 1/2　cup (1 stick) butter or margarine
>
> 2　squares (2 ounces) unsweetened chocolate
>
> 1　pound (3 1/2 to 4 cups) confectioners' sugar
>
> 1/2　cup half-and-half
>
> 1　teaspoon vanilla extract
>
> 4　medium bananas
>
> 2　tablespoons lemon juice

1. Preheat oven to 350°F. Place paper liners into 24 standard (2 1/2-inch) muffin cups. Prepare, bake and cool cupcakes following package directions for basic recipe.

2. For frosting,* melt butter and chocolate in heavy saucepan over low heat. Remove from heat. Add confectioners' sugar alternately with half-and-half, mixing until smooth after each addition. Beat in vanilla extract. Add more confectioners' sugar to thicken or half-and-half to thin as needed.

3. Using small paring knife, remove cone-shaped piece from top center of each cupcake. Dot top of each cone with frosting. Frost top of each cupcake spreading frosting down into cone-shaped hole. Slice bananas and dip in lemon juice. Stand three banana slices in each hole. Set cone-shaped pieces, pointed side down, on banana slices.

Makes 24 cupcakes

> Tip *Or use 1 can DUNCAN HINES® Creamy Home-Style Classic Chocolate Frosting.*

Lemon Poppy Seed Cupcakes

Cupcakes

- **1 package DUNCAN HINES® Moist Deluxe® Lemon Supreme Cake Mix**
- **3 eggs**
- **1⅓ cups water**
- **⅓ cup vegetable oil**
- **3 tablespoons poppy seeds**

Lemon Frosting

- **1 container (16 ounces) DUNCAN HINES® Creamy Home-Style Classic Vanilla Frosting**
- **1 teaspoon grated lemon peel**
- **¼ teaspoon lemon extract**
- **3 to 4 drops yellow food coloring**

1. Preheat oven to 350°F. Place paper liners into 30 standard (2½-inch) muffin cups.

2. For cupcakes, combine cake mix, eggs, water, oil and poppy seeds in large bowl. Beat at medium speed with electric mixer 2 minutes. Fill paper liners half full. Bake 18 to 21 minutes or until toothpick inserted into centers comes out clean. Cool in pans 5 minutes. Remove to cooling racks. Cool completely.

3. For lemon frosting, combine frosting, lemon peel and lemon extract in small bowl. Tint with yellow food coloring to desired color. Frost cupcakes.

Makes 30 cupcakes

Tip *Coat lemon strips with granulated sugar for a quick, sophisticated garnish.*

Angel Almond Cupcakes

    1 **package DUNCAN HINES®**
       Angel Food Cake Mix

1¼ **cups water**

    2 **teaspoons almond extract**

    1 **container DUNCAN HINES® Creamy**
       Home-Style Classic Vanilla Frosting

      Pastel-colored sprinkles, for garnish (optional)

1. Preheat oven to 350°F. Place foil or paper liners into 30 standard (2½-inch) muffin cups.

2. Combine cake mix, water and almond extract in large bowl. Beat at low speed with electric mixer until moistened. Beat at medium speed 1 minute. Fill muffin cups two-thirds full. Bake 20 to 25 minutes or until golden brown, cracked and dry on top. Remove from muffin pans; cool completely. Frost cupcakes and decorate with sprinkles.

Makes 30 to 32 cupcakes

Chocolate Peanut Butter Cups

1 package **DUNCAN HINES®** Moist Deluxe® Swiss Chocolate Cake Mix

1 container **DUNCAN HINES®** Creamy Home-Style Classic Vanilla Frosting

½ cup creamy peanut butter

15 miniature peanut butter cup candies, wrappers removed, cut in half vertically

1. Preheat oven to 350°F. Place paper liners into 30 standard (2½-inch) muffin cups.

2. Prepare, bake and cool cupcakes following package directions for basic recipe.

3. Combine frosting and peanut butter in medium bowl. Stir until smooth. Frost cupcakes. Decorate with peanut butter cup candy, cut-side down.

Makes 30 servings

Tip *You can substitute Duncan Hines® Moist Deluxe® Devil's Food, Dark Chocolate Fudge or Butter Recipe Fudge Cake Mix.*

Berry Surprise Cupcakes

1   package **DUNCAN HINES® Moist Deluxe® White Cake Mix**

3   **egg whites**

1⅓ **cups water**

2   **tablespoons vegetable oil**

3   **sheets (0.5 ounce each) strawberry chewy fruit snacks**

1   **container DUNCAN HINES® Creamy Home-Style Classic Vanilla Frosting**

2   **pouches (0.9 ounce each) chewy fruit snack shapes, for garnish (optional)**

1. Preheat oven to 350°F. Place paper liners into 24 standard (2½-inch) muffin cups.

2. Combine cake mix, egg whites, water and oil in large bowl. Beat at low speed with electric mixer until moistened. Beat at medium speed 2 minutes. Fill paper liners half full.

3. Cut each fruit snack sheet into nine equal pieces. (You will have three extra pieces.) Place fruit snack piece on top of batter in each cup. Pour remaining batter equally over each. Bake 18 to 23 minutes or until toothpick inserted into centers comes out clean. Cool in pans 5 minutes. Remove to cooling racks. Cool completely. Frost cupcakes. Decorate with fruit snack shapes, if desired.

Makes 24 cupcakes

Berry Surprise Cake

Grease and flour 13×9×2-inch pan. Prepare cake following package directions for basic recipe. Pour half the batter into prepared pan. Place four fruit snack sheets evenly on top. Pour remaining batter over all. Bake and cool as directed on package. Frost and decorate as directed.

Captivating Caterpillar Cupcakes

   1   package **DUNCAN HINES**® Moist Deluxe®
         White Cake Mix

   3   **egg whites**

 1⅓   **cups water**

   2   **tablespoons vegetable oil**

  ½   **cup star decors, divided**

   1   container **DUNCAN HINES**® Creamy
         Home-Style Classic Vanilla Frosting

       Green food coloring

   6   **chocolate sandwich cookies, finely crushed**

  ½   **cup candy-coated chocolate pieces**

  ⅓   **cup assorted jelly beans**

       Assorted nonpareil decors

1. Preheat oven to 350°F. Place paper liners into 24 standard (2½-inch) muffin cups.

2. Combine cake mix, egg whites, water and oil in large bowl. Beat at low speed with electric mixer until moistened. Beat at medium speed 2 minutes. Fold in ⅓ cup star decors. Fill paper liners about half full. Bake 18 to 23 minutes or until toothpick inserted into centers comes out clean. Cool in pans 5 minutes. Remove to cooling racks. Cool completely.

3. Tint frosting with green food coloring. Frost cupcakes. Sprinkle ½ teaspoon chocolate cookie crumbs onto each cupcake. Arrange four candy-coated chocolate pieces on cupcake to form caterpillar body. Place jelly bean at one end to form head. Attach remaining star and nonpareil decors with dots of frosting to form eyes. Repeat with remaining cupcakes.

Makes 24 cupcakes

Surprise-Filled Cupcakes

1 package **DUNCAN HINES®** Moist Deluxe®
   Dark Chocolate Fudge Cake Mix

1 **jar (7 ounces) marshmallow crème, divided**

1 **container DUNCAN HINES®** Creamy
   Home-Style Dark Chocolate
   Fudge Frosting

½ **cup confectioners' sugar**

2½ **teaspoons milk**

1. Preheat oven to 350°F. Place paper liners into 24 standard (2½-inch) muffin cups.

2. Prepare, bake and cool cupcakes following package directions for basic recipe.

3. Reserve 2 tablespoons marshmallow crème; set aside. Place remaining marshmallow crème in decorating bag fitted with large star tip. Push tip into center of each cupcake about 1 inch deep. Squeeze bag for 5 to 7 seconds to fill cupcake.

4. Frost cupcakes. Combine reserved marshmallow crème and confectioners' sugar in small bowl. Add milk, 1 teaspoon at a time, stirring until smooth. Place in small resealable plastic food storage bag. Cut one corner off bag. Squeeze icing over each cupcake to decorate.

Makes 24 cupcakes

Tip   *For an extra surprise, tint the marshmallow crème filling with a few drops of food coloring.*

For the Cookie Jar

Quick Peanut Butter Chocolate Chip Cookies

  1 **package DUNCAN HINES® Moist Deluxe® Classic Yellow Cake Mix**
  ½ **cup creamy peanut butter**
  ½ **cup (1 stick) butter or margarine, softened**
  2 **eggs**
  1 **cup milk chocolate chips**

1. Preheat oven to 350°F. Grease baking sheets.

2. Combine cake mix, peanut butter, butter and eggs in large bowl. Beat at low speed with electric mixer until well blended. Stir in chocolate chips.

3. Drop by rounded teaspoonfuls onto prepared baking sheets. Bake 9 to 11 minutes or until lightly browned. Cool 2 minutes on baking sheets. Transfer to cooling racks to cool completely.

Makes about 4 dozen cookies

Tip *Crunchy peanut butter can be substituted for the creamy peanut butter.*

Pinwheel Cookies

⅟₂ **cup shortening**

⅓ **cup plus 1 tablespoon butter, softened, divided**

2 **egg yolks**

⅟₂ **teaspoon vanilla extract**

1 **package DUNCAN HINES® Moist Deluxe® Fudge Marble Cake Mix**

1. Combine shortening, ⅓ cup butter, egg yolks and vanilla extract in large bowl. Mix at low speed with electric mixer until blended. Set aside cocoa packet from cake mix. Gradually add cake mix. Blend well.

2. Divide dough in half. Add cocoa packet and remaining 1 tablespoon butter to one half of dough. Knead until well blended and chocolate-colored.

3. Roll out yellow dough between two pieces of waxed paper into 18×12×⅛-inch rectangle. Repeat with chocolate dough. Remove top pieces of waxed paper from chocolate and yellow doughs. Place yellow dough directly on top of chocolate dough and press lightly. Remove remaining layers of waxed paper. Roll up jelly-roll fashion, beginning at wide side. Refrigerate 2 hours.

4. Preheat oven to 350°F. Grease baking sheets.

5. Cut dough into ⅛-inch slices. Place 1 inch apart on prepared baking sheets. Bake 9 to 11 minutes or until lightly browned. Cool 5 minutes on baking sheets. Transfer to cooling racks to cool completely.

Makes about 3½ dozen cookies

Chocolate Oat Chewies

1   package **DUNCAN HINES®** Moist Deluxe®
Devil's Food Cake Mix

1⅓ cups old-fashioned oats, uncooked

1   cup flaked coconut, toasted and divided

¾ cup (1½ sticks) butter or margarine, melted

2   eggs, beaten

1   teaspoon vanilla extract

5   bars (1.55 ounces each) milk chocolate, cut
into rectangles

1. Preheat oven to 350°F.

2. Combine cake mix, oats, ½ cup coconut, butter, eggs and vanilla extract in large bowl. Beat at low speed with electric mixer until well blended. Cover and chill 15 minutes.

3. Shape dough into 1-inch balls. Place balls 2 inches apart on ungreased baking sheets. Bake 12 minutes or until tops are slightly cracked. Remove from oven. Press one milk chocolate rectangle into center of each cookie. Sprinkle with remaining ½ cup coconut. Transfer to cooling racks to cool completely.

Makes about 4½ dozen cookies

Orange Pecan Gems

1 package **DUNCAN HINES®** Moist Deluxe®
    Orange Supreme Cake Mix

1 container (8 ounces) vanilla low-fat yogurt

1 egg

2 tablespoons butter or margarine, softened

1 cup finely chopped pecans

1 cup pecan halves

1. Preheat oven to 350°F. Grease baking sheets.

2. Combine cake mix, yogurt, egg, butter and chopped pecans in large bowl. Beat at low speed with electric mixer until blended. Drop by rounded teaspoonfuls 2 inches apart onto prepared baking sheets. Press pecan half into center of each cookie. Bake 11 to 13 minutes or until golden brown. Cool 1 minute on baking sheets. Transfer to cooling racks to cool completely. Store in airtight container.

Makes about 4½ dozen cookies

Easy Lemon Cookies

   1 package **DUNCAN HINES® Moist Deluxe®
   Lemon Supreme Cake Mix**

   2 **eggs**

   ½ **cup vegetable oil**

   1 **teaspoon grated lemon peel**

   1 **cup pecan halves, for garnish**

1. Preheat oven to 350°F.

2. Combine cake mix, eggs, oil and lemon peel in large bowl. Stir until well blended. Drop by rounded teaspoonfuls 2 inches apart onto ungreased baking sheets. Press pecan half into center of each cookie. Bake 9 to 11 minutes or until edges are light golden brown. Cool 1 minute on baking sheets. Remove to wire racks. Cool completely. Store in airtight container.

Makes about 4 dozen cookies

Tip *You can substitute whole almonds or walnut halves for the pecan halves.*

Coconut Clouds

2⅔ cups flaked coconut, divided

1 package **DUNCAN HINES®** Moist Deluxe® **Classic Yellow Cake Mix**

1 **egg**

½ **cup vegetable oil**

¼ **cup water**

1 **teaspoon almond extract**

1. Preheat oven to 350°F. Reserve 1⅓ cups coconut in medium bowl.

2. Combine cake mix, egg, oil, water and almond extract in large bowl. Beat at low speed with electric mixer. Stir in remaining 1⅓ cups coconut. Drop rounded teaspoonful of dough into reserved coconut. Roll to cover lightly. Place on ungreased baking sheet. Repeat with remaining dough, placing balls 2 inches apart. Bake 10 to 12 minutes or until light golden brown. Cool 1 minute on baking sheets. Transfer to cooling racks to cool completely. Store in airtight container.

Makes about 3½ dozen cookies

Pecan Date Bars

Crust

⅓ **cup shortening**

1 **package DUNCAN HINES® Moist Deluxe® Classic White Cake Mix**

1 **egg**

Topping

1 **package (8 ounces) chopped dates**

1¼ **cups chopped pecans**

1 **cup water**

½ **teaspoon vanilla extract**

Confectioners' sugar

1. Preheat oven to 350°F. Grease and flour 13×9×2-inch pan.

2. For crust, cut shortening into cake mix with pastry blender or two knives until mixture resembles coarse crumbs. Add egg; stir well. (Mixture will be crumbly.) Press mixture into bottom of prepared pan.

3. For topping, combine dates, pecans and water in medium saucepan. Bring to a boil. Reduce heat; simmer until mixture thickens, stirring constantly. Remove from heat. Stir in vanilla extract. Spread date mixture evenly over crust. Bake 25 to 30 minutes. Cool completely. Dust with confectioners' sugar. Cut into bars.

Makes about 32 bars

Double Chocolate Chewies

1 package **DUNCAN HINES® Moist Deluxe®
Butter Recipe Fudge Cake Mix**

2 **eggs**

½ **cup (1 stick) butter or margarine, melted**

1 **package (6 ounces) semisweet
chocolate chips**

1 **cup chopped nuts**

Confectioners' sugar, for garnish (optional)

1. Preheat oven to 350°F. Grease bottom only of 13×9×2-inch pan.

2. Combine cake mix, eggs and melted butter in large bowl. Stir until thoroughly blended. (Mixture will be stiff.) Stir in chocolate chips and nuts. Press mixture evenly into prepared pan. Bake 25 to 30 minutes or until toothpick inserted into center comes out clean. Do not overbake. Cool completely. Cut into bars. Dust with confectioners' sugar, if desired.

Makes about 36 bars

Double-Nut Chocolate Chip Cookies

- 1 package **DUNCAN HINES®** Moist Deluxe® **Classic Yellow Cake Mix**
- ½ **cup (1 stick) butter or margarine, melted**
- 1 **egg**
- 1 **cup semisweet chocolate chips**
- ½ **cup finely chopped pecans**
- 1¼ **cups sliced almonds, divided**

1. Preheat oven to 375°F. Grease baking sheets.

2. Combine cake mix, butter and egg in large bowl. Beat at low speed with electric mixer until just blended. Stir in chocolate chips, pecans and ¼ cup almonds. Shape rounded tablespoonfuls of dough into balls. Place remaining 1 cup almonds in shallow bowl. Press tops of balls into almonds. Place 1 inch apart on prepared baking sheets.

3. Bake 9 to 11 minutes or until lightly browned. Cool 2 minutes on baking sheets. Transfer to cooling racks to cool completely.

Makes about 3 dozen cookies

Dazzling Desserts

Cappuccino Bon Bons

1	package **DUNCAN HINES®** Family-Style **Chewy Fudge Brownie Mix**
2	eggs
⅓	cup water
⅓	cup vegetable oil
1½	tablespoons instant coffee
1	teaspoon ground cinnamon
	Whipped topping, for garnish
	Ground cinnamon, for garnish

1. Preheat oven to 350°F. Place foil mini cupcake liners on cookie sheet.

2. Combine brownie mix, eggs, water, oil, instant coffee and cinnamon. Stir with spoon until well blended, about 50 strokes. Fill each cupcake liner with 1 measuring tablespoon batter. Bake 12 to 15 minutes or until toothpick inserted into centers comes out clean. Cool completely. Garnish with whipped topping and a dash of cinnamon. Refrigerate until ready to serve.

Makes about 40 bon bons

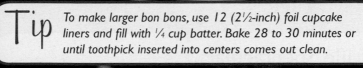

Tip To make larger bon bons, use 12 (2½-inch) foil cupcake liners and fill with ¼ cup batter. Bake 28 to 30 minutes or until toothpick inserted into centers comes out clean.

Trifle Spectacular

1 package **DUNCAN HINES® Moist Deluxe®
Devil's Food Cake Mix**

1 can (14 ounces) sweetened condensed milk

1 cup cold water

1 package (4-serving size) vanilla-flavor
instant pudding and pie filling mix

2 cups whipping cream, whipped

2 tablespoons orange juice

2½ cups sliced fresh strawberries

1 pint fresh raspberries

2 kiwifruit, peeled and sliced

1½ cups frozen nondairy whipped topping,
thawed, for garnish

Mint leaves, for garnish (optional)

1. Preheat oven to 350°F. Grease and flour two 9-inch round cake pans.

2. Prepare, bake and cool cake following package directions for basic recipe. Cut one cake layer into 1-inch cubes. Freeze remaining cake layer for another use.

3. Combine sweetened condensed milk and water in large bowl. Stir until blended. Add pudding mix. Beat until thoroughly blended. Chill 5 minutes. Fold whipped cream into pudding mixture.

4. To assemble, spread 2 cups pudding mixture into 3-quart trifle dish (or 3-quart clear glass bowl with straight sides). Arrange half the cake cubes over pudding mixture. Sprinkle with 1 tablespoon orange juice. Layer with 1 cup strawberry slices, half the raspberries and one-third of kiwifruit slices. Repeat layers. Top with remaining pudding mixture. Garnish with whipped topping, remaining ½ cup strawberry slices, kiwifruit slices and mint leaves, if desired.

Makes 10 to 12 servings

Tip Since the different layers contribute to the beauty of this recipe, arrange the fruit pieces to show attractively along the sides of the trifle dish.

Chocolate Almond Biscotti

1 package **DUNCAN HINES**® Moist Deluxe®
    Dark Chocolate Fudge Cake Mix

1 **cup all-purpose flour**

½ **cup (1 stick) butter or margarine, melted**

2 **eggs**

1 **teaspoon almond extract**

½ **cup chopped almonds**

White chocolate, melted (optional)

1. Preheat oven to 350°F. Line 2 baking sheets with parchment paper.

2. Combine cake mix, flour, butter, eggs and almond extract in large bowl. Beat at low speed with electric mixer until well blended; stir in almonds. Divide dough in half. Shape each half into 12×2-inch log; place logs on prepared baking sheets.

3. Bake 30 to 35 minutes or until toothpick inserted into centers comes out clean. Remove logs from oven; cool on baking sheets 15 minutes. Using serrated knife, cut logs into ½-inch slices. Arrange slices on baking sheets. Bake 10 minutes. Transfer to cooling racks; cool completely.

4. Dip one end of each biscotti into melted white chocolate, if desired. Allow white chocolate to set at room temperature before storing biscotti in airtight container.

Makes about 2½ dozen cookies

Chocolate Petits Fours

 1 package **DUNCAN HINES® Moist Deluxe®
Dark Chocolate Fudge Cake Mix**

 1 package (7 ounces) pure almond paste

 ½ cup seedless red raspberry jam

 3 cups semisweet chocolate chips

 ½ cup vegetable shortening

1. Preheat oven to 350°F. Grease and flour 13×9×2-inch pan.

2. Prepare, bake and cool cake following package directions for basic recipe. Remove from pan. Cover and store overnight.

3. For petits fours, level top of cake. Trim ¼-inch strip of cake from all sides. (Be careful to make straight cuts.) Cut cake into small squares, rectangles or triangles with serrated knife. Cut round and heart shapes with 1½- to 2-inch cookie cutters. Split each individual cake horizontally into two layers.

4. For filling, cut almond paste in half. Roll half the paste between two sheets of waxed paper to ⅛-inch thickness. Cut into same shapes as individual cakes. Repeat with second half of paste. Warm jam in small saucepan over low heat until thin. Remove top of one cake. Spread ¼ to ½ teaspoon jam on inside of each cut surface. Place one almond paste cutout on bottom layer. Top with second half of cake, jam side down. Repeat with remaining cakes.

5. For glaze, place chocolate chips and shortening in 4-cup glass measuring cup. Microwave on MEDIUM (50% power) 2 minutes; stir. Microwave 2 minutes longer on MEDIUM; stir until smooth. Place three assembled cakes on cooling rack over bowl. Spoon chocolate glaze over each cake until top and sides are completely covered. Transfer to waxed paper when glaze has stopped dripping. Repeat process until all cakes are covered. (Return chocolate glaze in bowl to glass measuring cup as needed; microwave on MEDIUM 30 to 60 seconds to thin.)

6. Place remaining chocolate glaze in resealable plastic food storage bag; seal. Place bag in bowl of hot water for several minutes. Dry with paper towel. Knead until chocolate is smooth. Cut one corner off bag. Drizzle or decorate top of each petit four. Let stand until chocolate is set. Store in single layer in airtight containers.

Makes 24 to 32 servings

Tip
To make cutting the cake into shapes easier, bake the cake one day before assembling.

Angel Strawberry Bavarian

- 1 package **DUNCAN HINES®** **Angel Food Cake Mix**
- 1 package (10 ounces) frozen sweetened sliced strawberries, thawed
- 1 package (4-serving size) strawberry-flavor gelatin
- 1 cup boiling water
- 2½ cups whipping cream, chilled, divided
- 2½ tablespoons confectioners' sugar
- ¾ teaspoon vanilla extract
- 4 fresh strawberries, sliced and fanned, for garnish

  Mint leaves, for garnish (optional)

1. Preheat oven to 375°F.

2. Prepare, bake and cool cake following package directions. Cut cake into 1-inch cubes. Drain thawed strawberries, reserving juice.

3. Combine gelatin and boiling water in small bowl. Stir until gelatin is dissolved. Add enough water to strawberry juice to measure 1 cup; stir into gelatin. Refrigerate until gelatin is slightly thickened. Beat gelatin until foamy.

4. Beat 1 cup whipping cream until stiff peaks form in large bowl. Fold into gelatin along with strawberries.

5. Place cake cubes and strawberry mixture into 10-inch tube pan, alternating layers. Press lightly. Cover. Refrigerate overnight.

6. Unmold cake onto serving plate. Beat remaining 1½ cups whipping cream, confectioners' sugar and vanilla extract until stiff peaks form. Frost sides and top of cake. Refrigerate until ready to serve. Garnish with fresh strawberries and mint leaves, if desired.

Makes 12 to 16 servings

Double Berry Layer Cake

> 1 package **DUNCAN HINES®** Moist Deluxe® Strawberry Supreme Cake Mix
>
> ⅔ cup strawberry jam
>
> 2½ cups fresh blueberries, rinsed, drained
>
> 1 container (8 ounces) frozen nondairy whipped topping, thawed
>
> **Fresh strawberry slices, for garnish**

1. Preheat oven to 350°F. Grease and flour two 9-inch round cake pans.

2. Prepare, bake and cool cakes following package directions for basic recipe.

3. Place one cake layer on serving plate. Spread with ⅓ cup strawberry jam. Arrange 1 cup blueberries on jam. Spread half the whipped topping to within ½ inch of cake edge. Place second cake layer on top. Repeat with remaining ⅓ cup strawberry jam, 1 cup blueberries and remaining whipped topping. Garnish with strawberry slices and remaining ½ cup blueberries. Refrigerate until ready to serve.

Makes 12 to 16 servings

Tip

For best results, cut cake with serrated knife; clean knife after each slice.

Index